String Bass
93SB

Doris Gazda & Albert Stoutamire

Level 2
TECHNIQUE AND PROGRAM MUSIC FOR STRING ORCHESTRA AND INDIVIDUAL INSTRUCTION

CONTENTS

Introduction 2
I Rhythm Review 3
II Major and Minor Fingering Patterns 4
III Intervals and Tuning 8
IV The Keys of D, C, and G Major 10
V Five Note Major & Minor Fingering Patterns 14
VI Minor Modes 16
VII Basic Bowing Styles 17
VIII Time and Rhythm Studies 20
IX Back Extension 24
X The Keys of F and B♭ Major with Relative Minors 26
XI Forward Extension 30
XII The Key of A Major 31
XIII Sixteenth Notes 32
XIV Harmonized Melodies 34
    1. America 34
    2. We Shall Overcome 35
    3. Amaryllis 36
    4. Menuetto 37
    5. Surprise Symphony Theme 38
    6. Military March 40
    7. American Fiddle Tune Medley 42
XV Harmonics and Vibrato 44
XVI Writing Music 46
Index .... Inside Back Cover

Spotlight on Strings, Level 2 is available for Violin, Viola, Cello, String Bass, Teacher Score/Keyboard.

ISBN 0-8497-3349-9

INTRODUCTION

By now you have discovered the joy of playing your instrument. Now it's time to continue with more opportunities to become an accomplished string player.

As you learned in Level 1, for you to be successful you must:

1. Try as hard as you can to do everything correctly.
2. Find a time and place to practice regularly at home.
3. Ask your family to listen to you play your pieces.
4. Remember to bring your instrument and music to school on your lesson day. Have a pencil with you, too.

Here are some reminders for caring for your string bass:

1. Keep it in the case or cover when you are not playing it. Push in the end pin and tighten the screw. Make sure your case is completely closed before picking it up.
2. Clean it with a soft cloth before you put it away.
3. Store it where it will not get too hot or cold.
4. Until you have learned to tune your instrument, ask your teacher to tune the strings. Also have your teacher check the bridge and other parts of the instrument for general maintenance.

Here are some reminders to help you care for your bow:

1. Each time you play your string bass, tighten your bow so that a pencil will just barely slide between the hair and the stick.
2. Rosin the bow about 10 times in one direction before you play.
3. Wipe off the stick and loosen the hair before you put the bow back into the case.
4. Do not touch the hair at any time.

Special Features in Spotlight on Strings, Level 2

IMPROVISING MUSIC

When you make up music and play it without writing it down, you are improvising. Sometimes you can improvise a few notes in the middle of a piece that is already composed. Other times, you may wish to make up melodies of your own. You will be given suggestions for improvising as you progress through **Spotlight on Strings, Level 2**. Use those suggestions as a starting place for your own ideas about where and when to improvise.

All of the great composers improvised music. Sometimes they wrote down their improvisations which then became compositions that you play today. One of the best ways to listen to improvisation today is in the field of jazz. Many great jazz string players play concerts and have made excellent recordings. Try improvising in many different ways and have a good time with it!

WRITING MUSIC

Writing music is a wonderful adventure. In **Spotlight on Strings, Level 2**, you will learn how to write music on the staff and will also have the opportunity to write your own compositions. You may wish to try writing more music than there is room for in this book. For that, you will need a manuscript book. Once you learn how to write music by hand, then you may wish to investigate the possibilities for writing music at the computer. There are many computer programs for writing music and you should seek advice and recommendations from your teacher before acquiring software for your computer. No matter if you compose with manuscript paper or computer, always play the music that you write so that you are sure it is written the way you want it to sound.

I RHYTHM REVIEW

Names	Notes	Rests	Duration in $\frac{4}{4}$, $\frac{3}{4}$, & $\frac{2}{4}$ Time Signatures
Whole	o	▬	four beats of sound or silence
Half	♩ or ♩	▬	two beats of sound or silence
Quarter	♩ or ♩	𝄽	one beat of sound or silence
Eighth	♪ or ♪	𝄾	1/2 beat of sound or silence
Two Eighths	♫	𝄽	one beat of sound or silence

Beats - Steady pulses felt or heard in music like ticks of a clock.

TIME SIGNATURES

$\frac{4}{4}$ $\left(\frac{4}{♩}\right)$ $\left(\frac{4}{𝄽}\right)$ four beats in a measure / a quarter note or quarter rest receives one beat

$\frac{2}{4}$ $\left(\frac{2}{♩}\right)$ $\left(\frac{2}{𝄽}\right)$ two beats in a measure / a quarter note or quarter rest receives one beat

$\frac{3}{4}$ $\left(\frac{3}{♩}\right)$ $\left(\frac{3}{𝄽}\right)$ three beats in a measure / a quarter note or quarter rest receives one beat.

Rhythm Studies

Play on each open string.
1. Arco on any pitch.
2. Left or right hand pizzicato.

1. Rhythm Study in $\frac{4}{4}$ Time

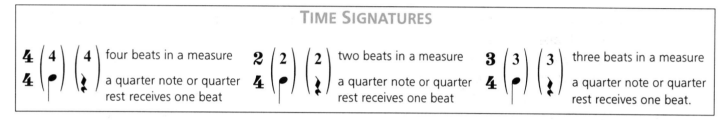

2. Rhythm Study in $\frac{2}{4}$ Time

In $\frac{2}{4}$ time, a whole rest receives two beats of silence.

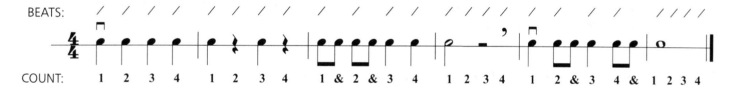

3. Rhythm Study in $\frac{3}{4}$ Time with a Pick-Up Note

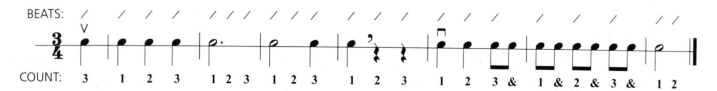

Improvising Music

Select $\frac{4}{4}$, $\frac{2}{4}$ or $\frac{3}{4}$ time signature and improvise a short rhythm on one open string.
Play your rhythm arco or pizzicato with any one note or combination of notes.
Teach it to your class.

II MAJOR & MINOR FINGERING PATTERNS

"I" means 1st position. "II" means 2nd position. Shift from 1st to 2nd position by moving the entire hand. Slide a finger along a string and the thumb along the back of the fingerboard. Keep the thumb approximately opposite the 2nd finger. A line following a position numeral (II———) means to stay in that position.

FIRST
POSITION (I)
Four fingers
down

SECOND
POSITION (II)
Four fingers
down

The distance from 1st finger to 4th finger is a whole step.
The distance from 1st finger to second finger or from second finger to 4th finger is a half step.

MAJOR FINGERING PATTERN

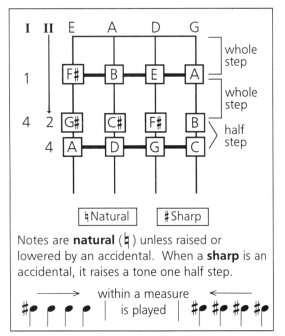

Notes are **natural** (♮) unless raised or lowered by an accidental. When a **sharp** is an accidental, it raises a tone one half step.

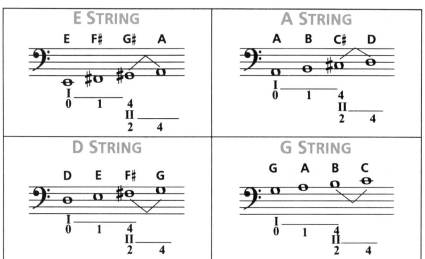

When placing the 4th finger on the string, always place the 3rd finger down with it.

MINOR FINGERING PATTERN

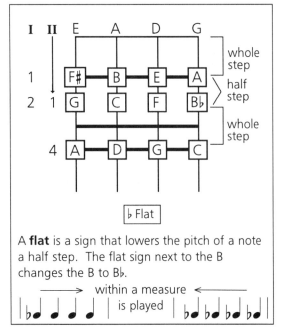

A **flat** is a sign that lowers the pitch of a note a half step. The flat sign next to the B changes the B to B♭.

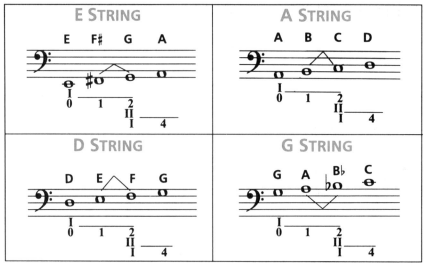

When placing the 4th finger on the string, always place the 3rd finger down with it.

Major and Minor Fingering Pattern Studies in 4/4 Time

1. G String - MAJOR Fingering Pattern

2. G String - MINOR Fingering Pattern

3. D String - MAJOR Fingering Pattern

4. D String - MINOR Fingering Pattern

> A natural (♮) before a note means that the note is neither flat nor sharp.

5. A String - MAJOR Fingering Pattern

6. A String - MINOR Fingering Pattern

7. E String - MAJOR Fingering Pattern   *Violin and Bass only.*

8. E String - MINOR Fingering Pattern   *Violin and Bass only.*

Improvising Music

Make up your own melody using either the major or minor fingering pattern on any one string. It may be different each time you play it.

MELODIES AND CHROMATIC STUDIES IN 2/4 TIME

Chromatic	Fermata
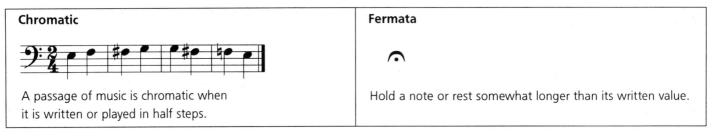	
A passage of music is chromatic when it is written or played in half steps.	Hold a note or rest somewhat longer than its written value.

1. Are You Sleeping?

Traditional Round

Improvising Music

Play *Are You Sleeping?* as written. Then change some of the quarter notes to sets of two eighth notes. Change the half notes any way you wish.

2. Bingo

American Camp Song

3. Major and Minor Fingering Patterns Combined

Chromatic patterns

a.

FINGERING: Slide the 2nd finger on the string.

b.

c.

4. Locomotive   *Play in 2nd position*

MELODIES IN 3/4 TIME

First and Second Endings

Play the first ending. Repeat.
Skip the first ending and play the second ending.

D.C. (*Da Capo*) al Fine

Go back to the beginning (*Da Capo*) and stop at the end (*Fine*).

FINGERING: 1_____ A line following a fingering means to keep that finger down.
② A fingering in a circle means place only that finger on the string.

1. Henry Martin

Scottish Ballad

2. Appalachian Folktune

*Always place the 3rd finger down with the 4th.

3. Surfing

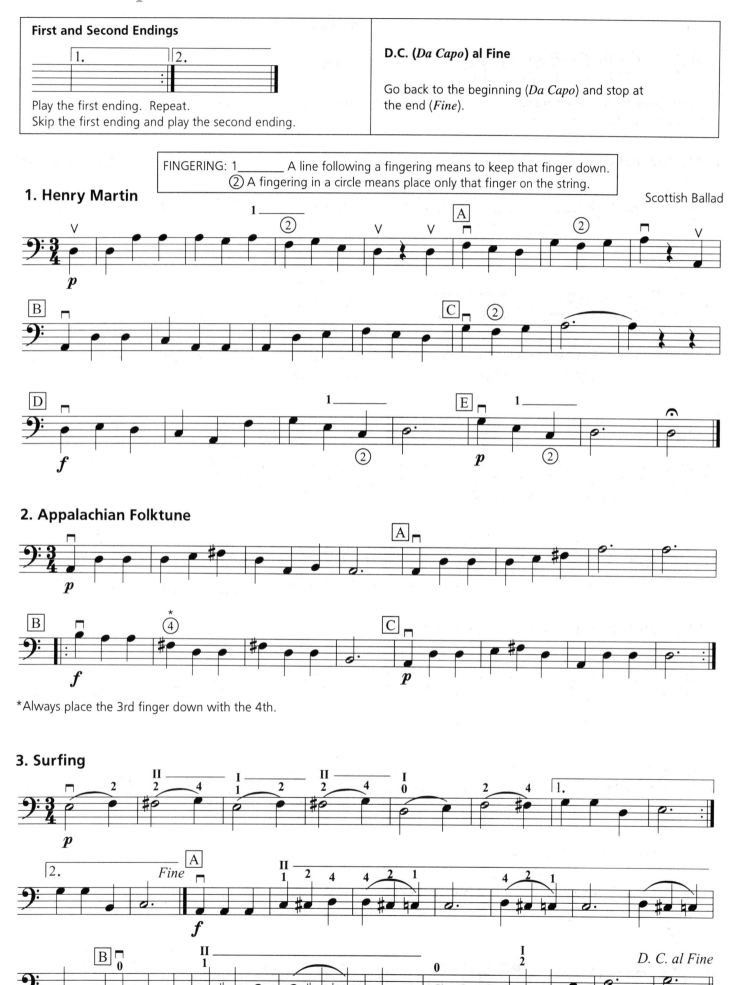

93SB

III INTERVALS AND TUNING

INTERVALS

An interval is the distance between two notes.

1. The smallest interval is called a minor second. A minor second interval is also called a half step.
   Half steps may be marked ⌒ or ⌄. The half steps you have been playing are:

a. Major Fingering Pattern

b. Minor Fingering Pattern

2. Two half steps equal a whole step.
   A whole step is also called an interval of a major second. Whole steps may be marked by ⌞⌟ or ⌜⌝.

a. Major Fingering Pattern

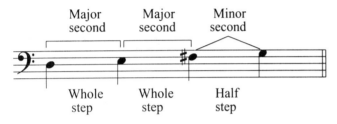

b. Minor Fingering Pattern

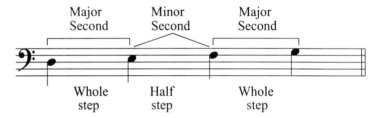

3. Intervals between the tones in a **D Major Scale**.

a. Whole Steps and Half Steps

b. Major Seconds and Minor Seconds

4. Lines and spaces are numbered in sequence. Intervals are also named in sequence.

a. Lines & spaces numbered beginning with "D."   **b. The intervals named from the key note "D."**

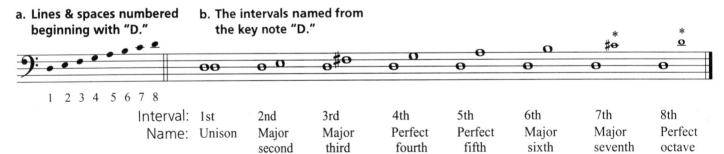

Interval:	1st	2nd	3rd	4th	5th	6th	7th	8th
Name:	Unison	Major second	Major third	Perfect fourth	Perfect fifth	Major sixth	Major seventh	Perfect octave

5. Intervals of a major scale (D Major):

* These are "cue" notes. You may listen to them or learn to play them by turning to pages 10 and 14.

Use the melodies on pages 6 and 7 to find and identify intervals of the major and minor second and the major third.

Writing Music

Turn to page 46, line #1. Follow the directions.

93SB

INTERVAL STUDIES

1. Perfect Fourths

2. Perfect Fifths

3. Octaves

TUNING

The strings on your instrument need to be tuned before each playing session. You will need a piano or a tuner to sound the correct reference pitch that corresponds to each of your open strings.

The machine screws are turned when you need to make large adjustments in pitch.

1. Hold the instrument with the peg box up and turned so that you are looking directly at the strings.
2. Sound the reference pitch, pluck the corresponding string and decide if the string sounds too high, too low, or just right.
3. With one hand plucking the string and the other hand turning the machine screw, tune the string to match the reference pitch.
    • To raise the pitch: Turn the top of the machine screw key away from you.
    • To lower the pitch: Turn the top of the machine screw key toward you.

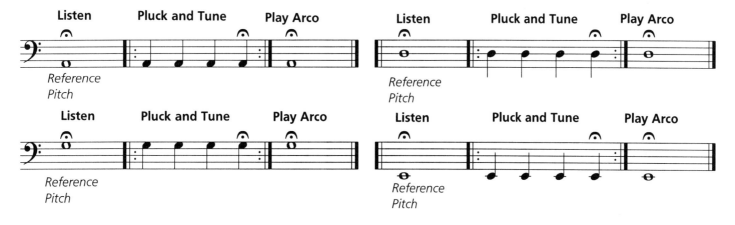

4. Tuning Tune

Make up your own *Tuning Tune*.

IV THE KEYS OF D, C, AND G MAJOR

A **key** is determined by sharps or flats called a **key signature**. The key signature appears at the beginning of a piece and tells which notes are to be raised or lowered for the entire piece.

A **scale** is a series of notes written or played stepwise in ascending or descending order with a specific sequence of whole steps and half steps determined by the key or key signature.

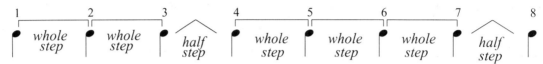

When the sequence is played in this order, it is called a **major scale**. The first and last notes ore called the **keynotes**.

KEY OF D MAJOR

In the key of **D Major**, F and C are sharped in the key signature. Play all F's as F♯ and all C's as C♯. The **scale of D Major** is in the key of D Major. It begins and ends on D. D is the keynote.

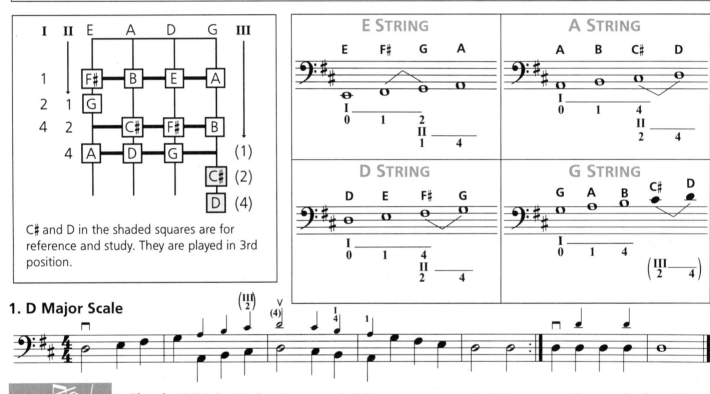

C♯ and D in the shaded squares are for reference and study. They are played in 3rd position.

1. D Major Scale

Improvising Music

Play the D Major Scale using two eighth notes on several of the tones. Change the bowing so that you include some slurs. Change the amount of bow you use. Alternate between forte and piano.

2. Finger Twister

3. Can-Can

Jacques Offenbach

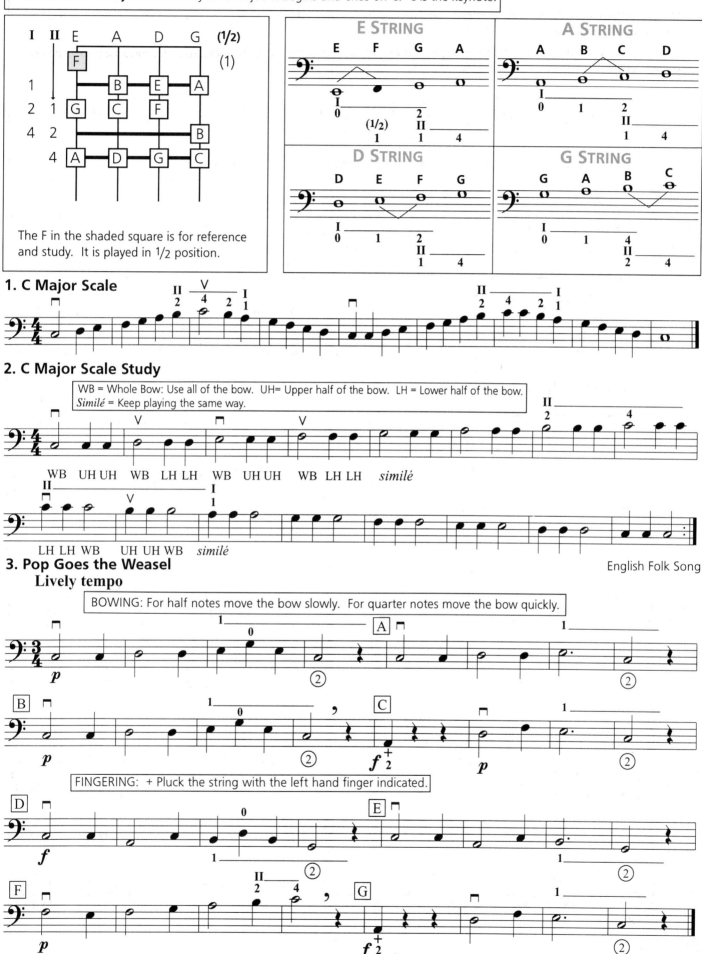

In the key of **C Major**, there are no sharps in the key signature.
The **scale of C Major** is in the key of C Major. It begins and ends on C. C is the keynote.

The F in the shaded square is for reference and study. It is played in 1/2 position.

1. C Major Scale

2. C Major Scale Study

WB = Whole Bow: Use all of the bow. UH= Upper half of the bow. LH = Lower half of the bow.
Similé = Keep playing the same way.

WB UH UH   WB LH LH   WB UH UH   WB LH LH   similé

LH LH WB   UH UH WB   similé

3. Pop Goes the Weasel
Lively tempo   English Folk Song

BOWING: For half notes move the bow slowly. For quarter notes move the bow quickly.

FINGERING: + Pluck the string with the left hand finger indicated.

Improvising Music

Play *Pop Goes the Weasel* as written. Play it again adding several notes to the melody wherever you feel they will sound good. Play your improvisation while everyone else plays the melody. The improvisation must "fit" with the melody.

93SB

KEY OF G MAJOR

In the key of **G Major**, F is sharped in the key signature. This means play all F's as F#. The **scale of G Major** is in the key of G Major. It begins and ends on G. G is the keynote.

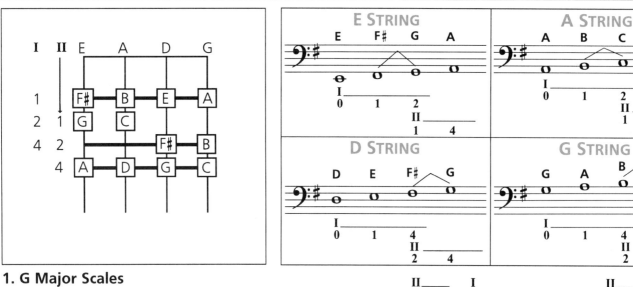

1. G Major Scales

2. Buffalo Gals

American Cowboy Song

3. Jonah and the Whale

American Spiritual

Turn to page 46, line #2. Follow the directions.

Writing Music

ARPEGGIOS IN D, C, AND G MAJOR

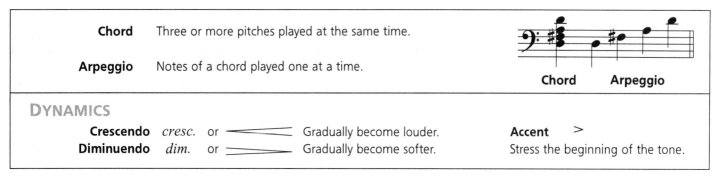

Chord	Three or more pitches played at the same time.	
Arpeggio	Notes of a chord played one at a time.	

DYNAMICS

Crescendo	*cresc.* or	Gradually become louder.	**Accent**
Diminuendo	*dim.* or	Gradually become softer.	Stress the beginning of the tone.

1. Building Arpeggios

2. Good Morning to You

American Camp Song

Improvising Music

Play *Good Morning to You*. Improvise with your own notes every time you come to a half note.

3. Nelly Bly–Duet

Stephen Foster

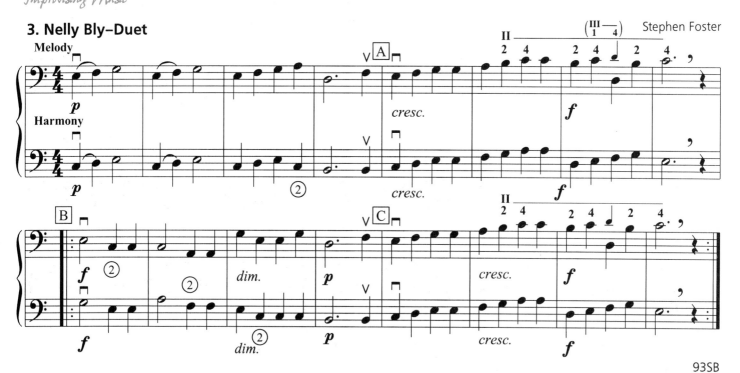

93SB

V FIVE NOTE MAJOR & MINOR FINGERING PATTERNS

FINGERING DIAGRAMS, NOTATION, AND ILLUSTRATIONS

MAJOR FINGERING PATTERN

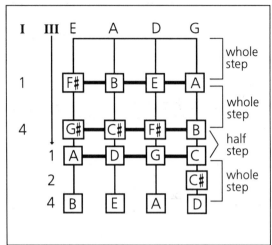

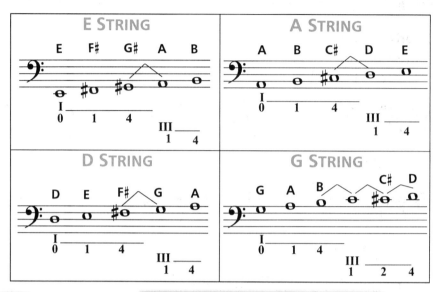

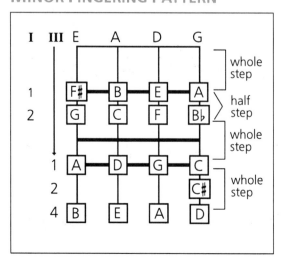

FIRST POSITION
FOUR FINGERS DOWN

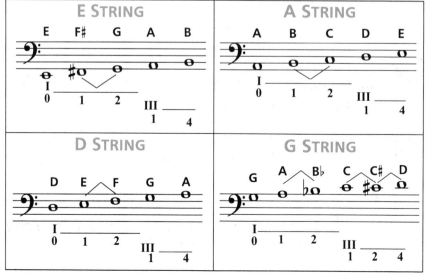

THIRD POSITION
FOUR FINGERS DOWN

"I" means first position. "III" means 3rd position. Shift 1st to 3rd position by moving the entire hand. Slide a finger along a string and the thumb along the back of the fingerboard. Keep the thumb approximately opposite the second finger. A line following a position numeral (III———) means stay in that position.

MINOR FINGERING PATTERN

MAJOR AND MINOR FINGERING PATTERN MELODIES

1. Shifting Position Exercise   *Cello and Bass only.*

2. Ode to Joy   Ludwig van Beethoven
Major Fingering Pattern*

3. The Birch Tree   Russian Folk Song
Minor Fingering Pattern*

* Except for the G string lines, all lines may be played in 1st position.

Improvise a melody on one string using the **major** fingering pattern. Play your melody again changing it to the **minor** fingering pattern.

Improvising Music

VI MINOR MODES

THE NATURAL MINOR SCALE AND MODAL MELODIES

The sequence of whole steps and half steps for a **natural minor** key is:

When the sequence is played in this order, it is called a **natural minor scale**. Another formula for the minor scale is to raise the sixth and seventh tones one half step.

1. Natural Minor Scale in E and Arpeggio

2. The Ghost of John - E Minor

English Folk Song

3. O Chanukah - A Minor

Israeli Folk Song

4. The Days of Knights - Duet in D Minor

Note: II½ position is introduced on page 30.

VII BASIC BOWING STYLES

LEGATO AND STACCATO

LEGATO - The notes sound connected.
   Détaché - Broad, alternating bow strokes smoothly connected.
   Slur - Two or more notes of different pitch played with one bow stroke.
STACCATO - The notes sound separated and are marked by a dot above or below the notehead.
   Martelé - Separated bow strokes. The bow remains **ON** the string.
   Spiccato - Separated bow strokes. The bow bounces **OFF** the string. Brush the string with the bow.

Theme and Variations

Improvise your own variation on the Hungarian folk song theme. Try to use at least two different bowing styles.

93SB

MELODIES WITH DÉTACHÉ, SLUR, MARTELÉ, AND SPICCATO BOWINGS

1. Rippling Rhythm   *Détaché and Slurs*

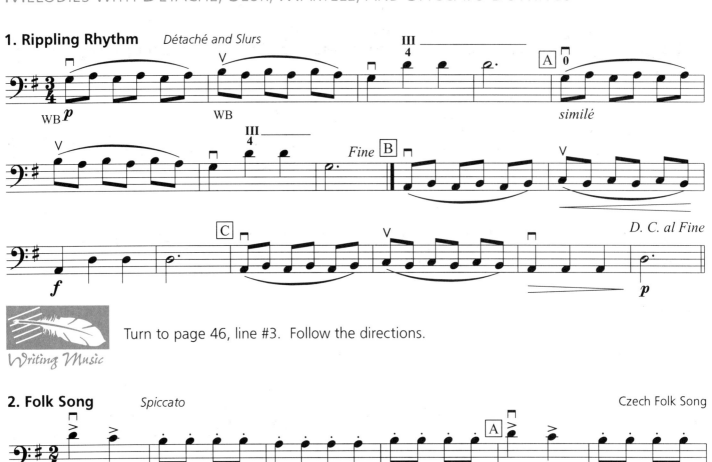

Turn to page 46, line #3. Follow the directions.

2. Folk Song   *Spiccato*   Czech Folk Song

3. Whiz Bang!   *Martelé and Détaché*

93SB

4. The Ferris Wheel   *Slurs and Détaché*

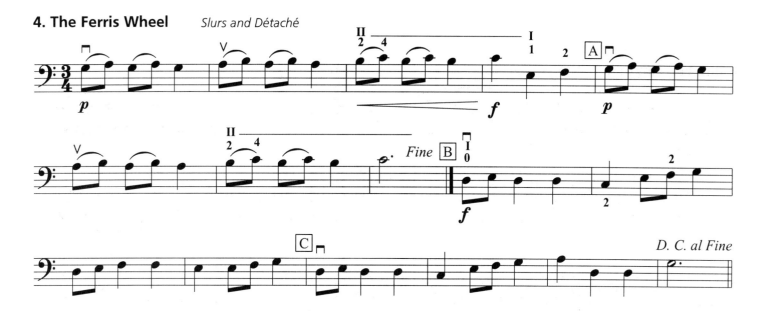

5. Calypso Duet

Martelé and Détaché

Note: The bow remains on the string except at the rest before letter B and at the end.

Writing Music

Turn to page 46, line #4. Follow the directions.

VIII TIME AND RHYTHM STUDIES

COMMON TIME AND CUT TIME

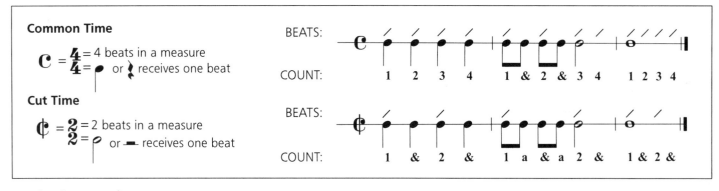

1. Rhythm Study
Play on each open string.

2. Ten Little Children
Spiritual

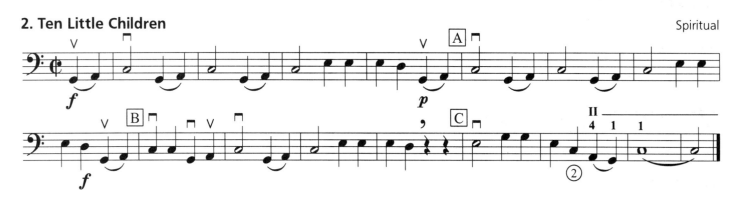

3. Knick-Knack Paddy Whack
American Folk Song

4. The Saints - Duet or Trio
New Orleans Jazz Tune

Improvising Music

Play *The Saints* as written. Improvise your own notes and rhythm between letters A and B and from letter C to the end.

DOTTED QUARTER AND EIGHTH NOTES

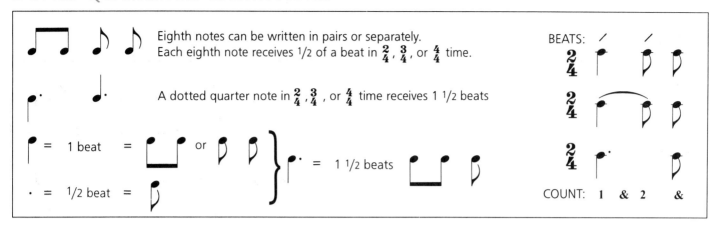

1. Rhythm Study   *Play on each open string.*

2. Etude   After learning each line, play the lines together as a duet.

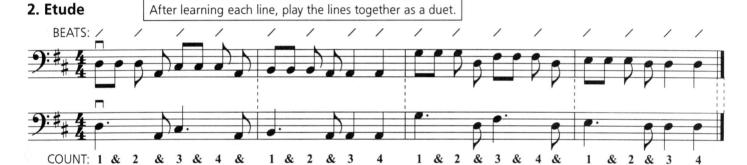

3. Deep and Wide   Spiritual

Improvising Music

Improvise on *Deep and Wide* while someone plays the keyboard accompaniment with you.

4. Auld Lang Syne   Scottish Folk Song

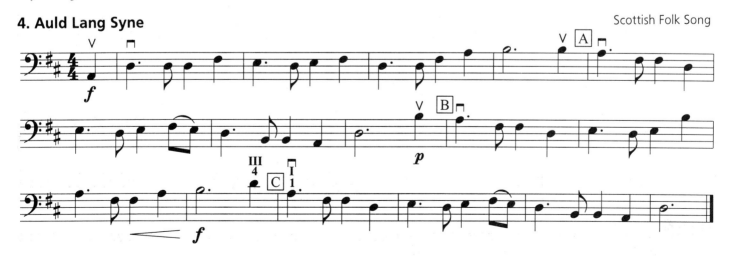

The Triplet

Duplet - A duplet is a group of two notes.

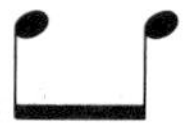

= 1 beat in 2/4, 3/4, or 4/4 time.

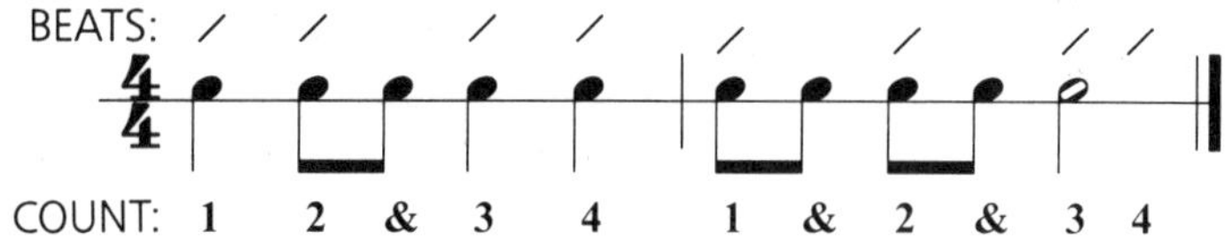

Triplet - A triplet is a group of three notes written in place of two notes of the same kind.

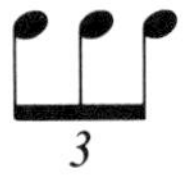

=1 beat in 2/4, 3/4, or 4/4 time.

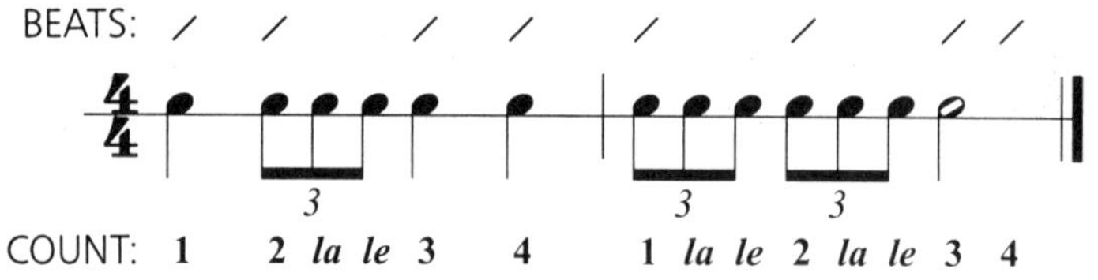

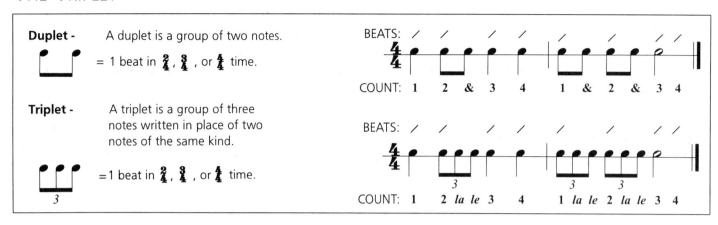

1. Rhythm Study *Play on each open string.*

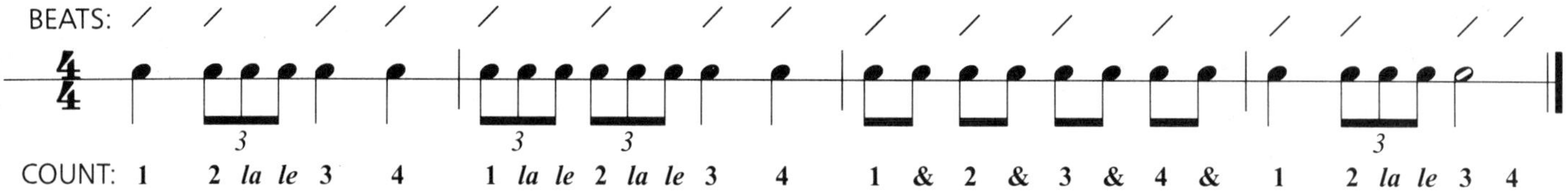

Writing Music

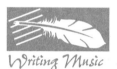

Turn to page 47, line #5. Follow the directions.

2. Scale Study

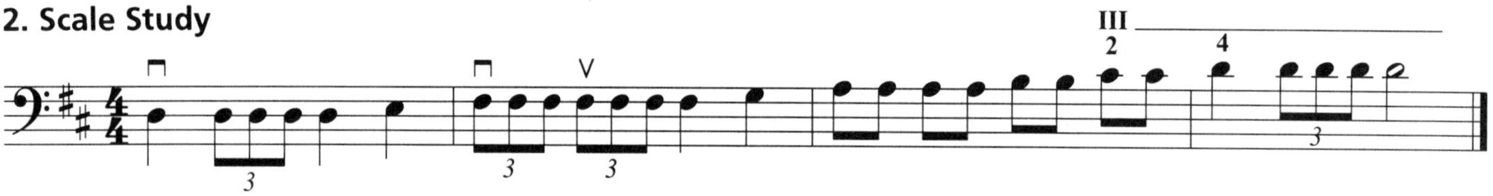

3. The Break Down

English Hornpipe

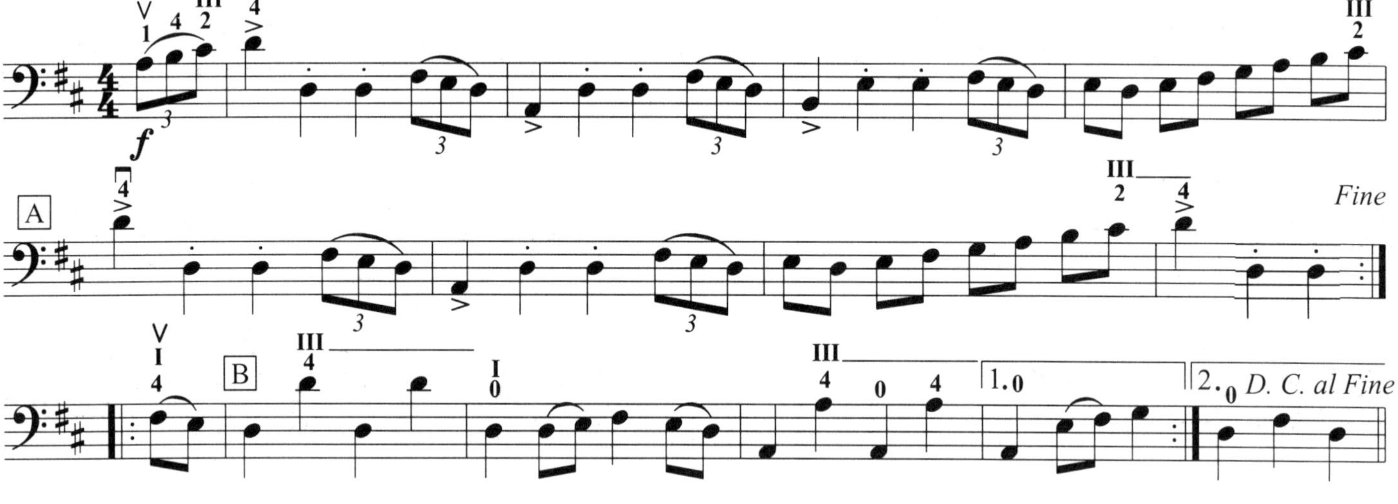

4. Nutcracker Fanfare - Duet or Trio

Peter Ilyich Tchaikovsky

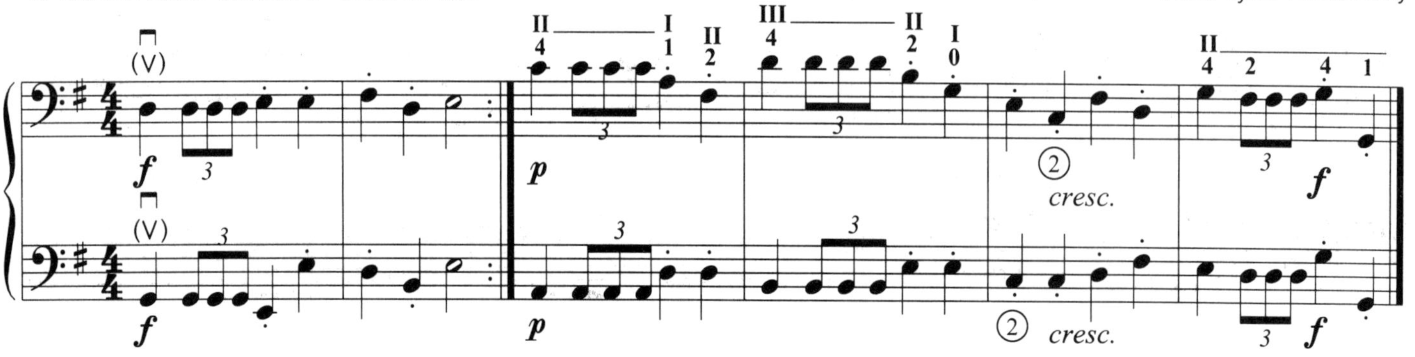

$\frac{6}{8}$ Time

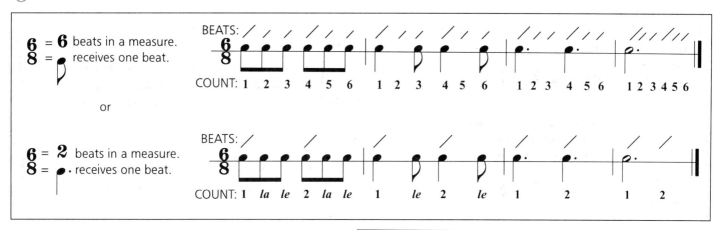

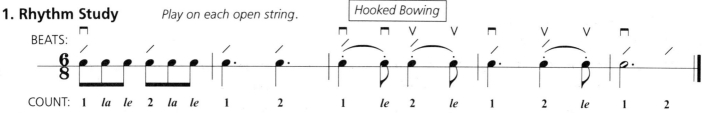

1. Rhythm Study
Play on each open string. Hooked Bowing

2. Scale Study
First time: 6 beats in a measure.
Second time: 2 beats in a measure.

Writing Music

Turn to page 47, line # 6. Follow the directions.

3. River Boat Song
Sea Chantey

4. El Gavilan
Mexican Folk Song

IX BACK EXTENSION

DIAGRAM, NOTATION, AND MELODIES

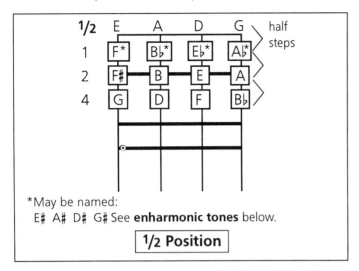

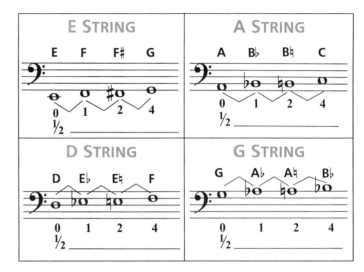

ENHARMONIC TONES

Enharmonic tones - Tones with two names which sound the same but are written differently.

1. Sliding Around

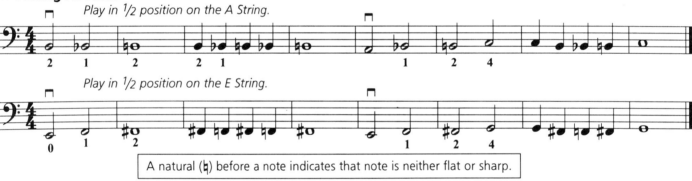

A natural (♮) before a note indicates that note is neither flat or sharp.

2. Marching Back

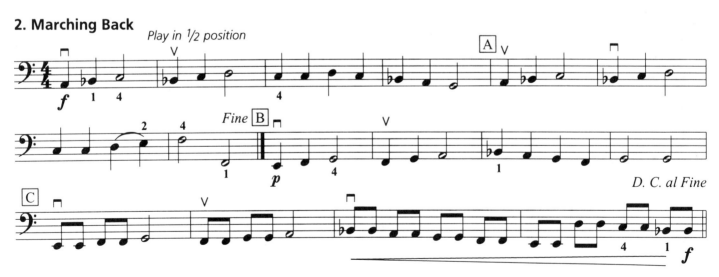

3. Jazz Blues Scale

Play the *Jazz Blues Scale* on page 24. Improvise any way you like using those notes.

Turn to page 47, line #7. Follow the directions.

+ = L. H. pizzicato

X THE KEYS OF F AND B♭ MAJOR WITH RELATIVE MINORS

F MAJOR

In the key of **F Major**, B is flat in the key signature. This means play all B's as B♭. The **scale of F Major** is in the key of F Major. It begins and ends on F. F is the keynote.

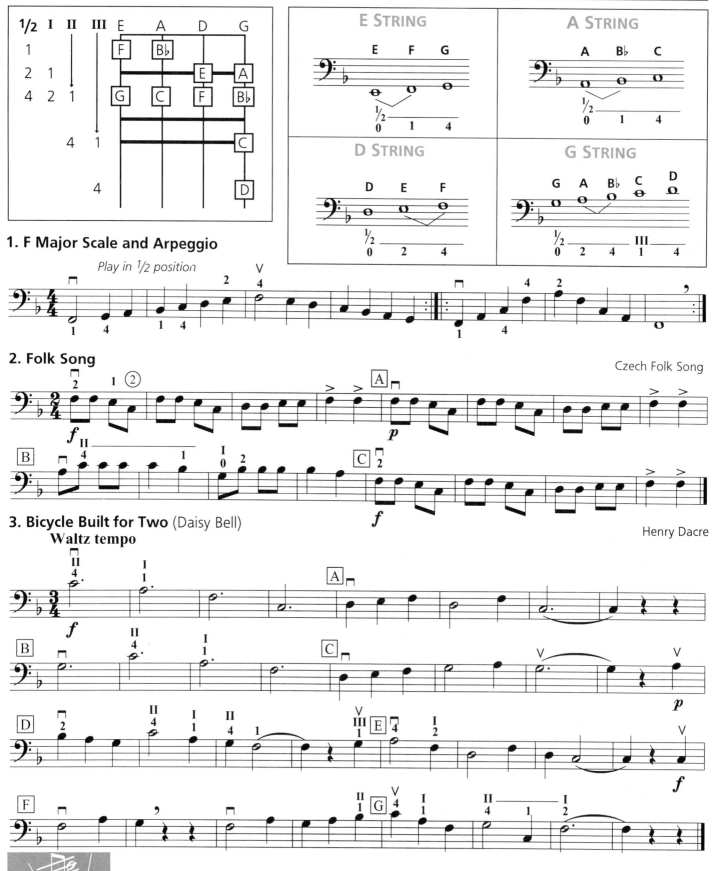

1. F Major Scale and Arpeggio

Play in ½ position

2. Folk Song

Czech Folk Song

3. Bicycle Built for Two (Daisy Bell)

Henry Dacre

Waltz tempo

Improvising Music

Play *Bicycle Built for Two* as written. Improvise your own notes every time you come to the last two measures of each line of music (the end of each phrase).

D Minor

In the key of **D Minor**, B is flat in the key signature. This means play all B's as B♭. The **scale of D Minor** is in the key of D Minor. It begins and ends on D. D is the keynote.

Major and minor keys with the same key signature are called "related keys."

1. D Minor Scale and Arpeggio

2. The Moldau Theme

Bedřich Smetana

Smooth and flowing

3. Canon

Hungarian Folk Song

4. When Johnny Comes Marching Home

Louis Lambert

With spirit

Writing Music

Turn to page 48, line #8. Follow the directions.

B♭ MAJOR

In the key of **B♭ Major**, B and E are flat in the key signature. This means play all B's and E's as B♭ and E♭. The **scale of B♭ Major** is in the key of B♭ Major. It begins and ends on B♭. B♭ is the keynote.

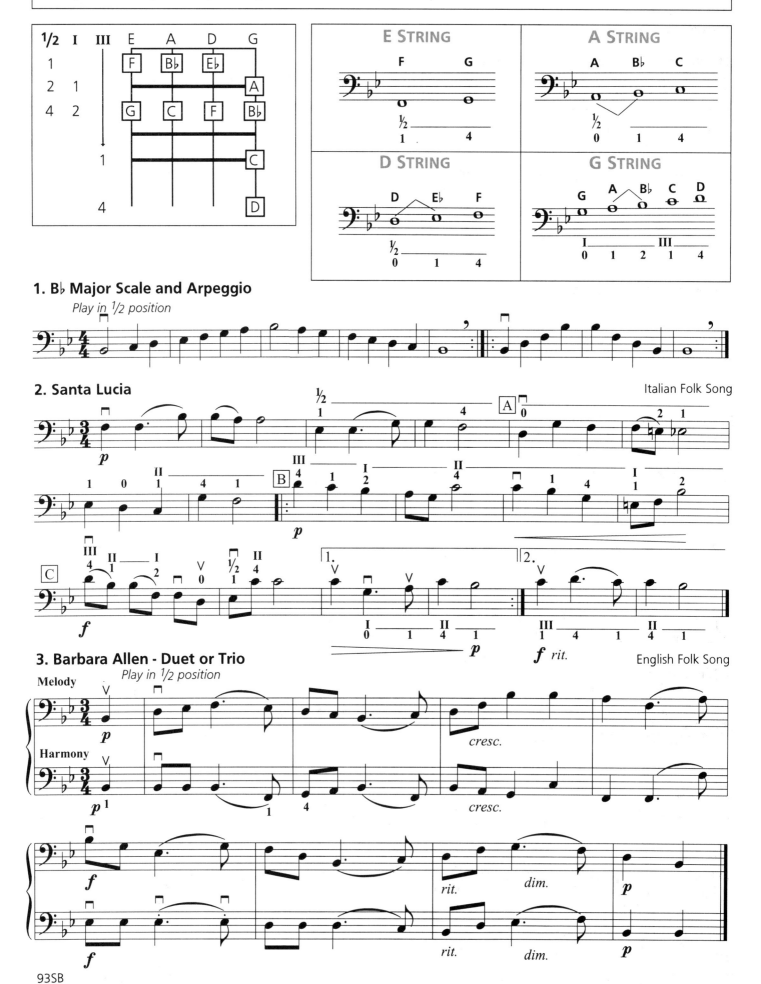

1. B♭ Major Scale and Arpeggio

2. Santa Lucia
Italian Folk Song

3. Barbara Allen - Duet or Trio
English Folk Song

G Minor

In the key of **G Minor**, B and E are flat in the key signature. This means play all B's and E's as B♭ and E♭. The **scale of G Minor** is in the key of G Minor. It begins and ends on G. G is the keynote.

Tempo - The speed at which music is performed.

Steady tempo indicators:
Allegro – Lively beat
Andante – Moderate walking beat

Changing tempo indicators:
Ritardando (*Rit.*) - Slow down the beat gradually.
Accelerando (*Accel.*) - Speed up the beat gradually.

a tempo - Play at the original speed.

1. G Minor Scale and Arpeggio

Play in ¹/₂ position

Play the *G Minor Scale and Arpeggio*. Improvise any way you like using these notes.

2. Hey! Ho! Nobody Home

Canon

Andante

3. At the Hour of Midnight (A la Media Noche)

Puerto Rican Carol

Allegro   *Play in ¹/₂ position*

4. Blues Rock

Andante

93SB

XI FORWARD EXTENSION
DIAGRAM, NOTATION, AND MELODIES

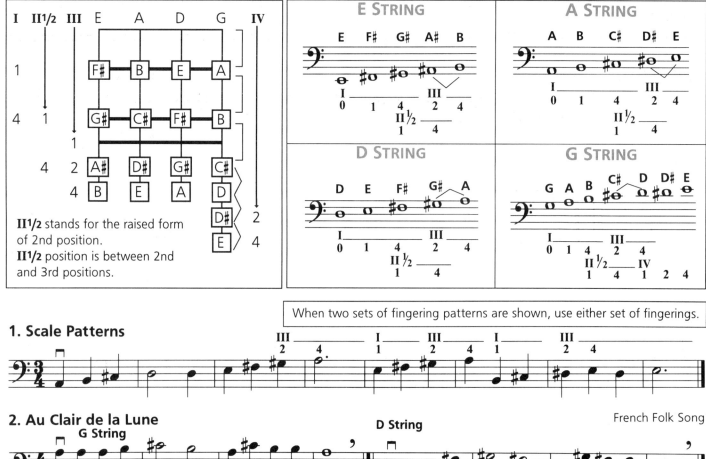

II1/2 stands for the raised form of 2nd position.
II1/2 position is between 2nd and 3rd positions.

When two sets of fingering patterns are shown, use either set of fingerings.

1. Scale Patterns

2. Au Clair de la Lune
French Folk Song

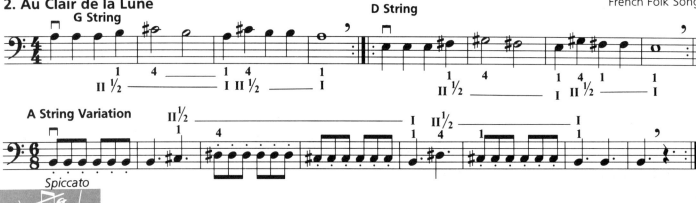

Improvise your own variation to *Au Claire de la Lune*.

3. Moveable Major Scale

This one-octave scale fingering may be used to play all major scales on any two adjacent strings. Always begin with the first finger.

4. Irish Reel
Traditional

A MAJOR   *XII THE KEY OF A MAJOR*

In the key of **A Major**, F, C, and G are sharped in the key signature. This means play all F's, C's, and G's as F♯, C♯, and G♯. The **scale of A Major** is in the key of A Major. It begins and ends on A. A is the keynote.

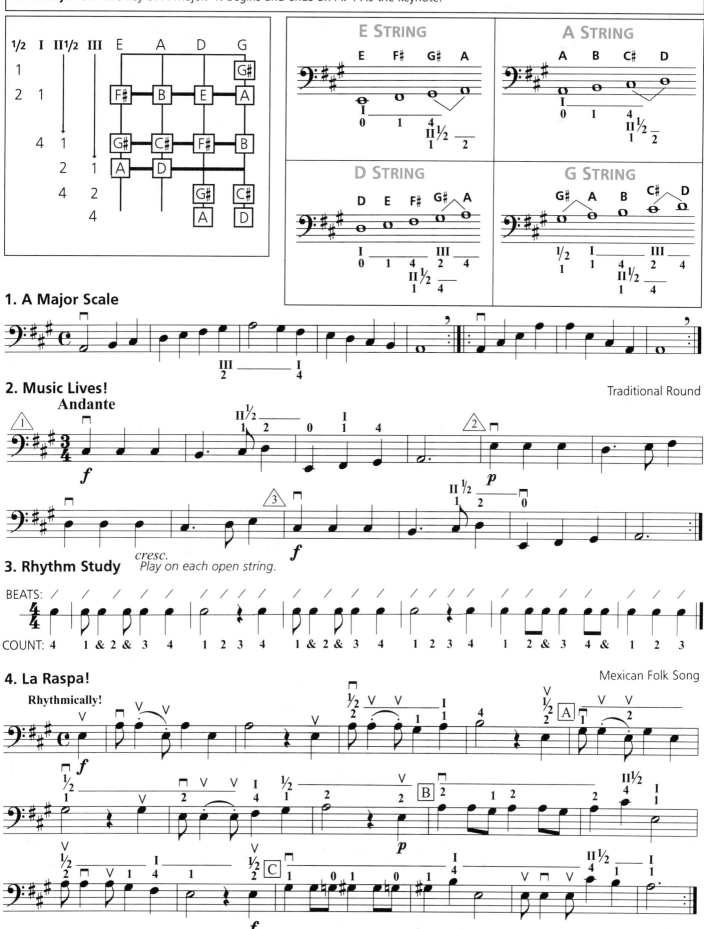

1. A Major Scale

2. Music Lives!

Andante

Traditional Round

3. Rhythm Study   *cresc.*   *Play on each open string.*

4. La Raspa!

Rhythmically!

Mexican Folk Song

Turn to page 48, line #9. Follow the directions.

93SB

XIII Sixteenth Notes

Sixteenth Notes ♫ = 1 beat   Each sixteenth note receives 1/4 of a beat.

1. Rhythm Study   *Play on each open string.*   Use whole bows on the quarter notes.

2. D Major Scale Study

3. Little Bells of Westminster   Round

Andante

Writing Music   Turn to page 48, line #10. Follow the directions.

4. Rhythm Study   *Play on each open string.*

5. Boil That Cabbage Down   Fiddle Tune

Allegro

Repeat twice

accel. last time

6. William Tell Theme   Gioacchino Rossini

Allegro

93SB

Play the melody of *Dinah Won't You Blow Your Horn* as written. Improvise your own notes when you get to the quarter notes and quarter rests.

XIV HARMONIZED MELODIES

AMERICA
Three Part Harmony*

*Each section may divide with half playing the melody part and half playing the ensemble part. When playing in a full ensemble for performance, all basses should play the ensemble part.

WE SHALL OVERCOME

Three Part Harmony*

MELODY PART

American Song

ENSEMBLE PART

*Each section may divide with half playing the melody part and half playing the ensemble part. When playing in a full ensemble for performance, all basses should play the ensemble part.

AMARYLLIS
Three Part Harmony*

MELODY PART

Henri Ghys

Use Martelé bowing for the staccato notes.

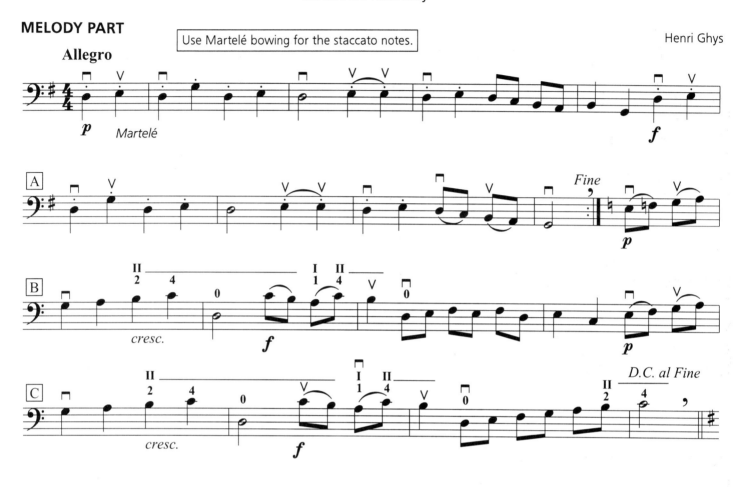

ENSEMBLE PART

Use Martelé bowing for the staccato notes.

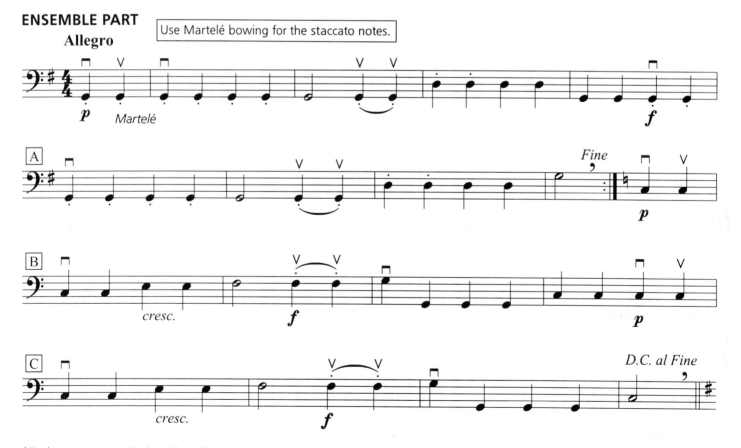

*Each section may divide with half playing the melody part and half playing the ensemble part. When playing in a full ensemble for performance, all basses should play the ensemble part.

93SB

Menuetto
Duet

Wolfgang Amadeus Mozart

Note: This arrangement may be played by all string instruments as an ensemble or by any two instruments as a duet.
*Light and lively, slightly slower than Allegro.

SURPRISE SYMPHONY THEME
Three Part Harmony*

MELODY PART

Franz Joseph Haydn

*Each section may divide with half playing the melody part and half playing the ensemble part. When playing in a full ensemble for performance, all basses should play the ensemble part.

(*Surprise Symphony* Theme, cont.)

ENSEMBLE PART

MILITARY MARCH
Three Part Harmony*

MELODY PART

Franz Schubert

*Each section may divide with half playing the melody part and half playing the ensemble part. When playing in a full ensemble
for performance, all basses should play the ensemble part.

(*Military March*, cont.)

ENSEMBLE PART

42

AMERICAN FIDDLE TUNE MEDLEY

Duet

Moderate Square Dance Tempo

"Turkey in the Straw"

Traditional

Note: This arrangement may be played by all string instruments as an ensemble or by any two instruments as a duet.

93SB

(*Medley*, cont.)

Arkansas Traveler

XV HARMONICS AND VIBRATO

LEARNING TO PLAY HARMONICS

Tones are produced on a string instrument by bowing or plucking:
1. **Open Strings**
2. **Stopped Tones** - Notes produced by pressing the string down with a finger
3. **Harmonic Tones** - Notes produced by lightly touching a string at a node

A **node** is a point where the string divides into harmonic segments.

1. The First Harmonic

Place your finger at the 1/2 node or halfway between the nut and the bridge. Lightly touch the string.

2. The Second Harmonic

Place your finger at the 1/3 node or 1/3 of the way from the nut to the bridge. Lightly touch the string.

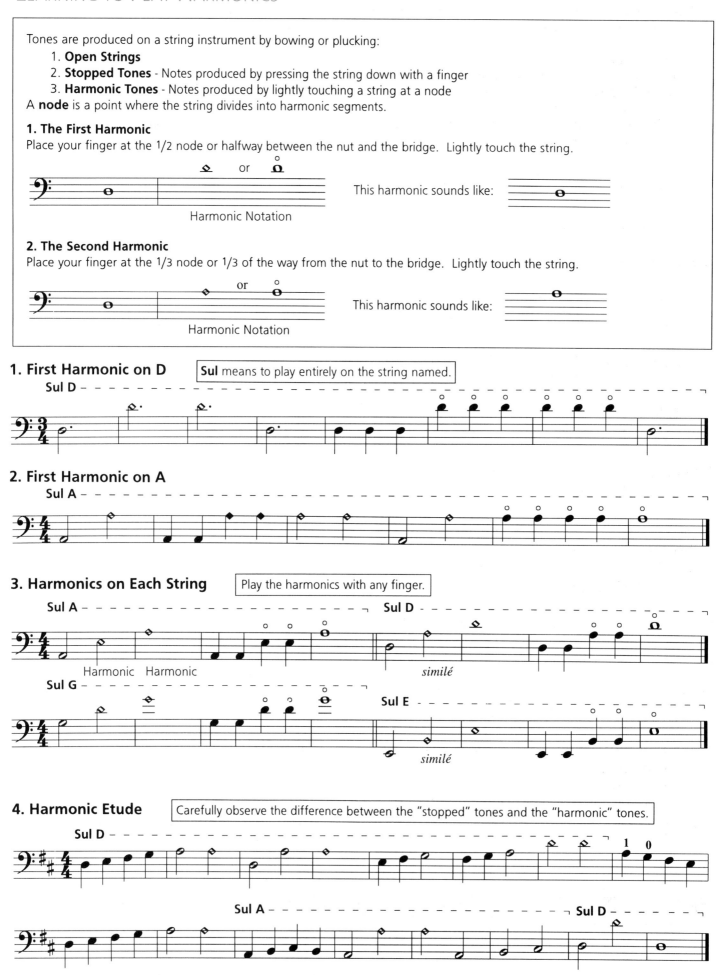

1. First Harmonic on D | **Sul** means to play entirely on the string named. |

2. First Harmonic on A

3. Harmonics on Each String | Play the harmonics with any finger. |

4. Harmonic Etude | Carefully observe the difference between the "stopped" tones and the "harmonic" tones. |

LEARNING TO PLAY WITH VIBRATO

Vibrato is a slight, constant change of pitch on sustained tones. It is used to enhance the tone and expressive qualities of a musical instrument. On a string instrument, it is produced by a steady back and forth motion of the finger, wrist, and arm.

Producing the vibrato motion:
1. Find and play the second harmonic (at the 1/3 node) with your first finger.
2. Keeping your thumb in place, slide your finger back about a half inch from the location of the harmonic and then return to the point where the harmonic is best produced. Your finger should feel as though it is polishing the string.
3. Continue the back and forth motion slowly at first. Increase the speed slightly keeping the hand relaxed and the motion steady. Fingers of the left hand touch the instrument in only two places:
   a) The thumb touches the neck of the instrument
   b) One finger at a time touches a string.
4. Try this motion with your 2nd, 3rd, and 4th fingers on the first harmonic (at the 1/2 node).

〰〰〰 means to produce the slow the vibrato motion

1. Sul D Vibrato
    Slide your finger back and forth only on the notes indicated. Use whole bows.

2. Sul A Vibrato
    Slide your finger back and forth only on the notes indicated. Use whole bows.

3. Continuing to make the harmonic tone, play #1 and #2 by moving your arm back and forth so that your finger is **rolling** on its tip.

4. Play #1 and #2 by **lightly pressing** the string to the fingerboard. You are now playing a stopped tone rather than a harmonic tone. Continue to move your arm back and forth so that the finger is **rolling** on its tip. Be sure that only one finger at a time touches the string and that the side of your left hand is not touching the neck of the instrument.

5. Move your hand a step at a time toward first position. Play a slow vibrato on each finger. Try this on all four strings.

6. Vibrato in First Position

7. Vibrato Etude Try to produce a slow vibrato on each half, dotted half, and whole note (except for open string notes).

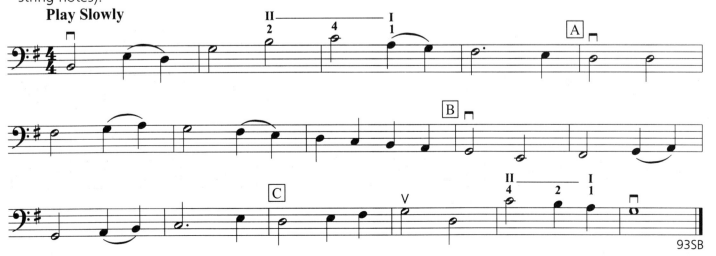

XVI WRITING MUSIC

1. Copy the ascending and descending D Major scale and name the notes. Reminder: notes placed on or above the middle line have stems going down and are positioned to the left of the notehead. Notes placed below the middle line have stems going up and are positioned to the right of the notehead.

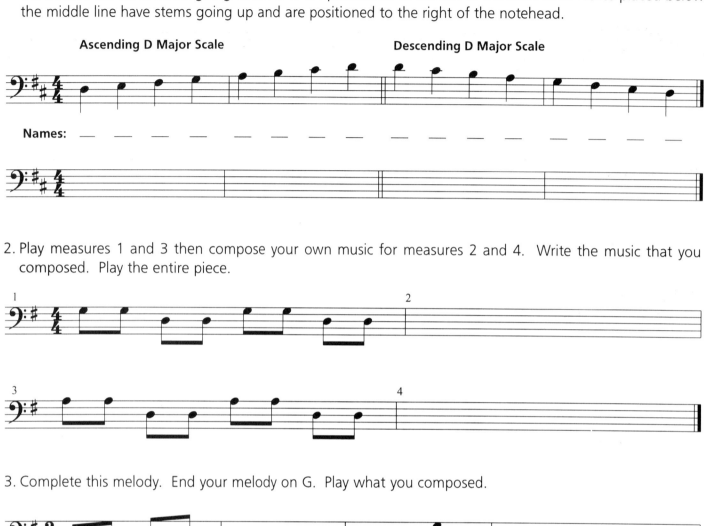

2. Play measures 1 and 3 then compose your own music for measures 2 and 4. Write the music that you composed. Play the entire piece.

3. Complete this melody. End your melody on G. Play what you composed.

4. Write your own melody using either the $\frac{2}{4}$ or the $\frac{3}{4}$ time signature in the key of C. Before you start composing, place the clef sign and time signature on the staff. Start and end your melody on C.

5. Write an ascending and descending C Major scale with a triplet for each tone of the scale in the $\frac{2}{4}$ time signature. Play what you have written.

ascending

descending

6. Copy measures 1 and 2 in measures 3 and 4. Compose your own music in measures 6, 7, and 8. Play your music.

7. Practice making flat, sharp, and natural signs.

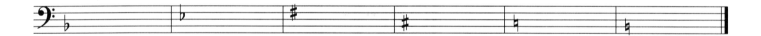

Copy measures 1, 2, and 3 in measures 5, 6, and 7. Play your music.

8. Write your own melody in the key of D Minor using the $\frac{2}{4}$, $\frac{4}{4}$, or $\frac{6}{8}$ time signature. Before you start to compose, place the clef sign, the key signature, and the time signature on the staff. Start and end your melody on D.

9. Write an ascending and a descending A Major scale in $\frac{4}{4}$ time. For each tone of the scale use this rhythm: ♪ ♪ ♪. Play the scale.

ascending

descending

10. Write your own melody in D Major using the $\frac{4}{4}$ time signature. Try to use a few groups of ♫♫ (four sixteenth notes). Before you begin composing, place the clef sign, the key signature, and the time signature on the staff. Start and end your melody on D.

Now you are ready to compose more music. You will need a music manuscript book for your composing. Think of the pieces you enjoyed playing. Look at how they were written. Try to write something similar. Think of the rhythms you like and use them in your compositions. If you are not satisfied with your composition, just turn the page and start over. GOOD LUCK!